A CENTURY *of*
SHEFFIELD

Mr Fred King working in the forge on a tilt hammer, *c.* 1950, at the Brightside Works of the famous Sheffield firm William Jessop and Sons Limited.

A CENTURY *of* SHEFFIELD

GEOFFREY HOWSE

SUTTON PUBLISHING

First published in the United Kingdom in 1999 by
Sutton Publishing Limited · Phoenix Mill
Thrupp · Stroud · Gloucestershire · GL5 2BU

British Library Cataloguing in Publication Data
A catalogue record for this book is available from the British Library.

ISBN 0-7509-2430-6

Front endpaper: The annual Horse Parade of William Stones Ltd, assembling outside the Cannon Brewery on 9 June 1902.
Back endpaper: The Super Tram, photographed from Sheaf Market, July 1999.
Half title page: The Moor in the 'swinging sixties'. This view, taken on 13 October 1967, shows many of the modern buildings constructed during that decade.
Title page: Mr John Thomas Ridge, gimlet maker, working in his smithy in Ecclesfield, shortly before his retirement at the age of ninety.

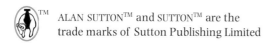

ALAN SUTTON™ and SUTTON™ are the trade marks of Sutton Publishing Limited

Typeset in 11/14pt Photina.
Typesetting and origination by
Sutton Publishing Limited.
Printed in Great Britain by
The Bath Press, Bath.

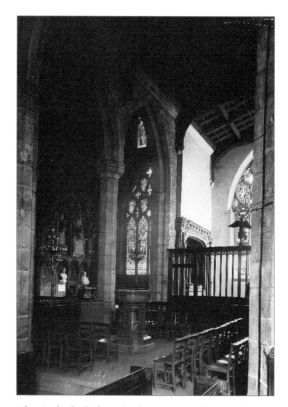

The Cathedral Church of St Peter and St Paul.

Contents

The Orchard Square clock – one of Sheffield's newest popular features – photographed on 16 July 1999.

Britain: A Century of Change

Children gathered around an early wireless set in the 1920s. The speed
and forms of communication were to change dramatically as the century
advanced. (*Barnaby's Picture Library*)

The delirious rejoicing at the news of the Relief of Mafeking, during the Boer War in May 1900, is a colourful historical moment. But, in retrospect, the introduction that year of the first motor bus was rather more important, signalling another major adjustment to town life. In the previous 60 years railway stations, post-and-telegraph offices, police and fire stations, gas works and gasometers, new livestock markets and covered markets, schools, churches, football grounds, hospitals and asylums, water pumping stations and sewerage plants had totally altered the urban scene, as the country's population tripled and over 70 per cent were born in or moved to the towns.

When Queen Victoria died in 1901, she was measured for her coffin by her grandson Kaiser Wilhelm, the London prostitutes put on black mourning and the blinds came down in the villas and terraces spreading out from the old town centres. These centres were reachable by train and tram, by the new bicycles and still newer motor cars, connected by the new telephone, and lit by gas or even electricity. The shops may have been full of British-made cotton and woollen clothing but the grocers and butchers were selling cheap Danish bacon, Argentinian beef, Australasian mutton, tinned or dried fish and fruit from Canada, California and South Africa. Most of these goods were carried in British-built-and-crewed ships, burning Welsh steam coal.

As the first decade moved on, the Open Spaces Act meant more parks, bowling greens and cricket pitches. The first state pensions came in, together with higher taxation and death duties. These were raised mostly to pay for the new Dreadnought battleships needed to maintain naval superiority over Germany, and deter them from war. But the deterrent did not work. The First World War transformed the place of women, as they took over many men's jobs. Its other legacies were the war memorials which joined the statues of Victorian worthies in main squares round the land. After 1918 death duties bit even harder and a quarter of England changed hands in a few years.

The multiple shop – the chain store – appeared in the high street: Sainsburys, Maypole, Lipton's, Home & Colonial, the Fifty Shilling Tailor, Burton, Boots, W.H. Smith. The shopper was spoilt for choice, attracted by the brash fascias and advertising hoardings for national brands like Bovril, Pears Soap, and Ovaltine. Many new buildings began to be seen,

Women working as porters on the Great Western Railway, Paddington, *c.* 1917. (*W.L. Kenning/ Adrian Vaughan Collection*)

such as garages, motor showrooms, picture palaces (cinemas), 'palais de dance', and the bow-windowed, pebble-dashed, tile-hung, half-timbered houses that were built as ribbon-development along the roads and new bypasses or on the new estates nudging the green belts.

During the 1920s cars became more reliable and sophisticated as well as commonplace, with developments like the electric self-starter making them easier for women to drive. Who wanted to turn a crank handle in the new short skirt? This was, indeed, the electric age as much as the motor era. Trolley buses, electric trams and trains extended mass transport and electric light replaced gas in the street and the home, which itself was groomed by the vacuum cleaner.

Father and child cycling past Buckingham Palace on VE Day, 8 May 1945. (*Hulton Getty Picture Collection*)

A major jolt to the march onward and upward was administered by the Great Depression of the early 1930s. The older British industries – textiles, shipbuilding, iron, steel, coal – were already under pressure from foreign competition when this worldwide slump arrived, cutting exports by half in two years and producing 3 million unemployed (and still rising) by 1932. Luckily there were new diversions to alleviate the misery. The 'talkies' arrived in the cinemas; more and more radios and gramophones were to be found in people's homes; there were new women's magazines, with fashion, cookery tips and problem pages; football pools; the flying feats of women pilots like Amy Johnson; the Loch Ness Monster; cheap chocolate and the drama of Edward VIII's abdication.

Things were looking up again by 1936 and unemployment was down to 2 million. New light industry was booming in the Home Counties as factories struggled to keep up with the demand for radios, radiograms, cars and electronic goods including the first television sets. The threat from Hitler's Germany meant rearmament, particularly of the airforce, which stimulated aircraft and aero engine firms. If you were lucky and lived in the south, there was good money to be earned. A semi-detached house cost £450, a Morris Cowley £150. People may have smoked like chimneys but life expectancy, since 1918, was up by 15 years while the birth rate had almost halved. The fifty-four hour week was down to forty-eight hours and there were 9 million radio licences by 1939.

In some ways it is the little memories that seem to linger longest from the Second World War: the kerbs painted white to show up in the blackout, the rattle of ack-ack shrapnel on roof tiles, sparrows killed by bomb blast, painting your legs brown and then adding a black seam

A family gathered around their television set in the 1950s. (*Hulton Getty Picture Collection*)

down the back to simulate stockings. The biggest damage, apart from London, was in the south-west (Plymouth, Bristol) and the Midlands (Coventry, Birmingham). Postwar reconstruction was rooted in the Beveridge Report which set out the expectations for the Welfare State. This, together with the nationalisation of the Bank of England, coal, gas, electricity and the railways, formed the programme of the Labour government in 1945. At this time the USA was calling in its debts and Britain was beggared by the war, yet still administering its Empire.

Times were hard in the late 1940s, with rationing even more stringent than during the war. Yet this was, as has been said, 'an innocent and well-behaved era'. The first let-up came in 1951 with the Festival of Britain and then there was another fillip in 1953 from the Coronation, which incidentally gave a huge boost to the spread of TV. By 1954 leisure motoring had been resumed but the Comet – Britain's best hope for taking on the American aviation industry – suffered a series of mysterious crashes. The Suez debacle of 1956 was followed by an acceleration in the withdrawal from Empire, which had begun in 1947 with the Independence of India. Consumerism was truly born with the advent of commercial TV and most homes soon boasted washing machines, fridges, electric irons and fires.

The *Lady Chatterley* obscenity trial in 1960 was something of a straw in the wind for what was to follow in that decade. A collective loss of inhibition seemed to sweep the land, as stately home owners opened up, the Beatles and the Rolling Stones transformed popular music, and retailing, cinema and the theatre were revolutionised. Designers, hairdressers, photographers and models moved into places vacated by an Establishment put to flight by the new breed of satirists spawned by *Beyond the Fringe* and *Private Eye*.

In the 1970s Britain seems to have suffered a prolonged hangover after the excesses of the previous decade. Ulster, inflation and union troubles were not made up for by entry into the EEC, North Sea Oil, Women's Lib or, indeed, Punk Rock. Mrs Thatcher applied the corrective in the 1980s, as the country moved more and more from its old manufacturing base over to providing services, consulting, advertising, and expertise in the 'invisible' market of high finance or in IT. Britain entertained the world with *Cats*, *Phantom of the Opera*, *Four Weddings and a Funeral*, *The Full Monty*, *Mr Bean* and the *Teletubbies*.

The post-1945 townscape has seen changes to match those in the worlds of work, entertainment and politics. In 1956 the Clean Air Act served notice on smogs and pea-souper fogs, smuts and blackened buildings, forcing people to stop burning coal and go over to smokeless sources of heat and energy. In the same decade some of the best urban building took place in the 'new towns' like Basildon, Crawley, Stevenage and Harlow. Elsewhere open warfare was declared on slums and what was labelled inadequate, cramped, back-to-back, two-up, two-down, housing. The new 'machine for living in' was a flat in a high-rise block. The architects and planners who promoted these were in league with the traffic engineers, determined to keep the motor car moving whatever the price in multi-storey car parks, meters, traffic wardens and ring roads.

Carnaby Street in the 1960s. (*Barnaby's Picture Library*)

The Millennium Dome at Greenwich, 1999. (*Michael Durnan/Barnaby's Picture Library*)

The old pollutant, coal smoke, was replaced by petrol and diesel exhaust, and traffic noise. Even in the back garden it was hard to find peace as motor mowers, then leaf blowers and strimmers made themselves heard, and the neighbours let you share their choice of music from their powerful new amplifiers, whether you wanted to or not. Fast food was no longer only a pork pie in a pub or fish-and-chips. There were Indian curry houses, Chinese take-aways and American-style hamburgers, while the drinker could get away from beer in a wine bar. Under the impact of television the big Gaumonts and Odeons closed or were rebuilt as multi-screen cinemas, while the palais de dance gave way to discos and clubs.

From the late 1960s the introduction of listed buildings and conservation areas, together with the growth of preservation societies, put a brake on 'comprehensive redevelopment'. Now the new risk at the end of the 1990s is that town centres may die, as shoppers are attracted to the edge-of-town supermarkets surrounded by parking space, where much more than food and groceries can be bought. The ease of the one-stop shop represents the latest challenge to the good health of our towns. But with care, ingenuity and a determination to keep control of our environment, this challenge can be met.

Sheffield: An Introduction

Sheffield, England's greenest city, is built on seven hills and five river valleys. With a population of over half a million, it is also England's fourth largest city. Its rivers played an important part in the development of the industries for which Sheffield has become world renowned. The five rivers are the Don, Sheaf, Rivelin, Loxley and Porter. Many districts and streets bear names associated with these all-important stretches of water. Many first-time visitors to Sheffield have a preconceived notion that they will be surrounded by dust and grime. They are often shocked because they find themselves visiting one of the cleanest industrial cities in Europe.

During the twentieth century Sheffield has changed dramatically. The photographs in this book show not only the changing face of Sheffield through the decades but also comparisons of then and now. Some things have changed very little, others beyond recognition. In 1914 Sheffield had a population of 450,000. At that time, over half the working population were engaged in the steel and cutlery producing industries. Many others worked in coal mines. One major advantage in having such diversity of heavy industry within one area has been the growth of unrivalled medical facilities. Research into various industrial and other illnesses at Sheffield's numerous medical institutions has resulted in the city being blessed with some of the finest teaching hospitals to be found anywhere in the United Kingdom.

Sheffield is a city of sport. It already had an enviable sporting record in staging events before the Sports Council named it as Britain's first National City of Sport in 1995. Soccer was born in Sheffield. Sheffield FC, founded on 24 October 1857, is the world's oldest football club. Matches were first played between teams made up of club members. Sheffield FC still exists and plays in local leagues. Sheffield produced the first soccer rule book when the area had 15 teams. In 1877 an agreement was made between the London Association and the Sheffield Association to use the same rules, which formed the basis of the rules still in use today. From those small beginnings, soccer has spread throughout the globe during the twentieth century to become the world's most popular sport. It has also continued to thrive in the city where it was conceived, a city which has two professional soccer teams, Sheffield Wednesday and Sheffield United.

At the end of the twentieth century Sheffield is known as the city with the best sports facilities in Britain. Many of these facilities were built for the World Student Games which were staged in Sheffield in 1991. These were one of the biggest sporting events ever held in Britain. The city invested £200 million in new sports facilities at Ponds Forge International Sports Centre, Don Valley Stadium and Hillsborough Leisure Centre. Graves Tennis and Leisure Centre has six indoor and twelve outdoor world-class courts. Major sporting events are regularly staged in Sheffield. As well as these large sporting complexes there are also several sports centres offering facilities to cater for all levels of ability. Sheffield Ski Village is the largest dry-ski centre in Europe and the city offers an enormous range of other sports and recreational facilities including golf, watersports of every conceivable kind, football, cricket, rugby, ice-skating, speedway,

Sheffield people were fond of commemorating important events. In this postcard view is the Coronation Pageant, which was featured in the Ecclesfield Hospital Parade in 1911.

The Wicker, one of the city's popular shopping areas, shown here in March 1989.

shooting, ten-pin bowling, bowls, riding, trekking, squash, badminton, athletics and climbing.

In keeping with the general trend in shopping facilities during the last twenty-five years, the city has made numerous changes and improved its facilities. In addition to department stores and shops in the city centre, there are a host of suburban shopping areas, each with its own identity. Crystal Peaks shopping and leisure centre is situated on the rural south-eastern fringe of the city. At Hillsborough, Sheffield Barracks has been converted to provide a busy shopping complex. At Broomhill, Crookes and Sharrow there are smaller areas of shops, public houses and restaurants, whereas Abbeydale Road is the antiques capital of the North, with dozens of shops offering a diverse range of goods. Eccleshall Road offers up-market specialist shops and Meadowhall, built on the site of a former steelworks, is a large American style shopping complex, which attracts more than 25 million shoppers a year.

The greater part of the twentieth century saw Sheffield's industries booming but, in more recent years, changes in technology and

Meadowhall, photographed
from the railway
interchange, July 1999.

production methods have meant that the industries, which for
centuries had been the biggest employers of Sheffielders, have had to
adapt to cater for modern trends in order to survive in a highly
competitive market place. In 1970 45,000 people were working in the
steel and cutlery industries in Sheffield. By the mid-1980s the number
had fallen to 12,000 and, in 1999, there are less than 8,000
Sheffielders engaged in this work. Modern methods of production
mean that only one man is needed where ten men were required
before. Surprising as it may seem, more tons of steel are produced in
Sheffield today than at any time during the history of the steel-making
industry in the city.

Sheffield built its world-wide reputation on cutlery-making and
steel production. As early as the fourteenth century Sheffield had
already established itself in the cutlery industry, when Geoffrey
Chaucer (*c.* 1340–1400) mentioned it in *The Canterbury Tales*, in

'The Reeve's Tale': 'A Sheffield thwitel [whittler] baar he in his hose'. By the nineteenth century Sheffield had become the world's foremost producer of cutlery, tools and silverware. By the beginning of the twentieth century the production of high-quality steel had become the major industry. Sheffield led the way in the production of alloy steels, such as manganese steel, an extremely tough wear-resistant steel, used extensively by the railway industry and in the production of armour plating; and silicon steel, used for electrical components. Stainless steel, by far the most important alloy steel, was first produced in 1913 by Harry Brearley at the Firth Brown Laboratories. It has been used in the cutlery industry and in everything from cooking utensils and kitchen equipment to the aeronautical and space industries. Like their illustrious predecessors, modern Sheffield companies are still household names and the best quality steel, tools, silver and holloware are still marked *Made in Sheffield.*

As England's greenest city, with over a third of its land lying inside Britain's first National Park, the Peak District National Park, Sheffield has as diverse a landscape as any city could wish. It contains moorland, forest, stretches of water, parks and gardens, as well as tree-lined suburbs. In the Botanical Gardens at Broomhill over 5,000 different species of plants are grown. Several parks provide nature trails and bird sanctuaries, including Rivelin Valley trail and Eccleshall Woods. Graves Park offers sculpture and a nature trail, as well as being the home of the Rare Breeds Centre, which is home to unusual breeds of cattle, sheep, pigs, ponies and other interesting animals.

The growth of Sheffield's two universities has improved the city's economy and given it further prestige. The building of the National Centre for Popular Music has also given something entirely new to the city and enhances the archive, exhibition and museum facilities available in the area. Employment has been the most significant factor affecting the lives of Sheffielders this century. By the mid-1990s Sheffield had over 3,000 small businesses, employing between 10 and 200 people each. As the century closes the industrial giants, which once employed the majority of Sheffielders, have largely disappeared. The legacy which has been left behind, and the institutions that their wealth created is steering Sheffield in a positive direction as the new millennium dawns. In the twentieth century Sheffield has grown from being a fledgling city – famous for cutlery and steel and, to the outside world, very little else – to becoming a world beater and a city in which its people can truly take pride.

Pond Street bus station and the Midland railway station, with Hyde Park flats dominating the skyline. The Super Tram can be seen above the railway station. This view was photographed in July 1999 from Arundel Gate.

Turn of the Century and the Edwardian Era

Commemorative postcard for the visit of the King Edward VII and Queen Alexandra in 1905.

Fitzalan Square, 1900. Despite the changes which have taken place throughout an entire century, Fitzalan Square has remained substantially the same, not least in its dimensions and atmosphere. Buildings around its fringes have been constructed and torn down again but the square itself has remained an important meeting place. In 1999, as in 1900, it is still a bustling square.

Workers at Samuel Staniforth's central cutlery works in 1900. The works were situated in Carver Street. This view shows the forging shop, where cutlery blanks were made. The works were opened in 1864 and operated until 1982.

Cutlery glazing, *c.* 1900.

Attercliffe Road, 16 May 1901.

A view down Fargate towards High Street, *c.* 1902. Marks & Spencer has occupied the site of the buildings on the right since the 1960s.

A view of Broomhill from Manchester Road in 1902. Many of the buildings on the right are substantially the same today.

First row—

R. Ferrier.
W. E. Hemingfield.
F. Thackery.

Second row—

J. Davis (Asst. Train
W. Layton.
A. Langley (Captain
J. Lyall.
T. Crawshaw.
H. Ruddlesden.
P. Frith (Trainer).

Third row—

V. S. Simpson.
H. Davis.
H. Chapman.
A. Wilson.
J. N. Mallock.
F. Spikesley.
G. Simpson.

Sheffield Wednesday League Team, League Champions 1902–3.

The central premises of Brightside and Carbrook Co-operative Society Limited, in 1903. The B & C Co-operative Society was incorporated in 1868 by Act of Parliament. The Central Stores contained the offices for the society. The entrance to the offices was by the door on the right of the photograph. To the right of the offices were a pair of wrought iron gates which allowed access to the loading bays and to the right of the gates were a pair of plate glass windows separated by a central doorway, the entrance to the drapery department.

Sheffield Barracks, Hillsborough, early 1900s. This distinctive landmark no longer serves a military purpose. In recent years the old barracks have been converted into a supermarket, public house, speciality shops and offices.

In this page of advertisements from Ecclesfield Parish Magazine, January 1903, it is very interesting to note the prices of goods being advertised. It is also reassuring to know that coffins could be made on the shortest notice – and at reasonable prices too! Who could ask for more?

The Moor, early 1900s.

This postcard view shows the interment of the Revd Dr Gatty in the churchyard of St Mary's Church, Ecclesfield. The celebrated Dr Gatty, author of several books, including *Life At One Living*, published in 1884, died on 20 January 1903. Dr Gatty was Vicar of Ecclesfield from 1839 until his death. He married Margaret, daughter of Alexander John Scott, Chaplain to Lord Nelson at the Battle of Trafalgar, who cradled the dying admiral in his arms. Dr Gatty shares the same burial vault as his father-in-law. The Gattys had ten children. Their second daughter, Juliana Ewing, was a noted children's author. Her invention of the Brownies inspired Baden-Powell to create a junior branch of the Girl Guides.

Pinstone Street viewed from the top of The Moor, *c.* 1905. The elegant railings on the right belong to St Paul's churchyard, now the site of the Peace Gardens. Sheffield Town Hall is in the background on the right. (See p. 120)

Electric tram No. 252 commenced service in 1905 and continued until 1923. It is seen here during the Edwardian period.

An early 1900s view of the Lyceum Theatre and Theatre Royal, two of the many fine theatres which Sheffield boasted at the beginning of the twentieth century.

Sheffield was granted a City Charter in 1893, although its parish church was not raised to cathedral status until 1914. The laying of the foundation stone of the University of Sheffield buildings in 1903 by the Lord Mayor of London, Sir Marcus Samuel Bt, later Lord Bearsted, marked a major stepping stone in the new city's transformation.

The completed University of Sheffield buildings, seen here in 1905.

Their Majesties King Edward Vll and Queen Alexandra arrive at the University of Sheffield, for the opening ceremony, on 12 July 1905.

Whenever there was an event to commemorate, Sheffield rose to the occasion and decorated the city streets in great style. This view of Lady's Bridge, shows just one of the many decorative arches which were erected for the visit of the King and Queen in 1905.

The royal procession makes its way through the city streets to the Town Hall.

Their Majesties' carriage arrives at the steps of Sheffield Town Hall, 12 July 1905.

Carbrook Hall, said to be Sheffield's most haunted building. It is situated on Attercliffe Common. Once standing in isolated splendour, it has been engulfed by the urbanisation which has taken place in the Lower Don Valley during the last 150 years. The hall has ancient origins. Late in the twelfth century the Blunts were living at Carbrook. During the late middle ages a fine timber-framed house was erected and in 1623 a new stone wing was added. By then a branch of the illustrious Bright family of Whirlow Hall were living at Carbrook. Carbrook Hall was used by the Roundheads during the siege of Sheffield Castle in 1644. The Brights were a wealthy, powerful and influential family in Sheffield, indeed there are many reminders throughout Sheffield of the Brights, including the district known as Brightside. On 26 February 1752 Mary Bright, daughter of Thomas Bright of Carbrook Hall, married Charles Watson Wentworth, 2nd Marquess of Rockingham, of Wentworth Woodhouse, near Rotherham. She was an heiress whose fortune made her a suitable match for Rockingham's high station. A much loved and respected Whig, Rockingham became Prime Minister twice and died in office in 1782. The marriage was not blessed with any children. On Lord Rockingham's death, his estates, which included the Bright legacy, passed to his nephew Earl Fitzwilliam. Mary, Marchioness of Rockingham, lived until December 1804. A descendent of the Bright's, Admiral Southerton, sold Carbrook Hall and its estate in 1819. By 1855 Carbrook Hall had become a public house. The estate and surrounding land was developed into what was to become the heart of the world's premier steel-making centre. The timber-framed portion of Carbrook Hall was demolished about 1800. The remaining 1623 block is listed Grade II*. Carbrook Hall is still a public house. Illustration drawn and etched by E. Blore.

Making crucible steel at William Jessop & Sons Limited, Brightside Works, *c.* 1904.

By the time these five photographs were taken, William Jessop and Sons Limited, established in Sheffield in 1774, had become synonymous with the making of high quality Sheffield Steel. Originally situated in the city itself, the firm moved to Brightside, which was then a pleasant country lane, in the 1820s. By the beginning of the twentieth century, Brightside presented an almost unbroken series of factories and steelworks, for a distance of over two miles. Jessops was the first firm to colonise Brightside and their premises became known as *the* Brightside Works. Other famous Sheffield firms who were operating from Brightside in the early years of this century were, Messrs. Vickers, Son and Maxim, John Brown & Co. and Charles Cammell & Co.

Jessops works had 18 'converting' furnaces, each of 20 to 25 tons capacity; 21 crucible furnaces, 28 steam and tilt hammers and 14 sets of rolls in the rolling mills. Approximately 1,500 men were employed at the works. At this time, the annual consumption of coal and coke was 80,000 tons and the annual production was 10,000 tons of Crucible steel and 22,000 tons of Siemens steel. The firm was the first in the world to produce cast-steel rams for battleships as well as steel rudder frames, stern frames, and propeller brackets made in a single piece. Jessops were contractors to the British Admiralty, as well as the navies of Russia, Spain and Japan. Jessop steel was exported all over the civilised world for the making of tools of every description, from those made to bore out cannons, or turn steel shafting to a depth of half an inch, down to the steel used for making sewing needles, fish hooks, clock and watch springs, cutlery, dies, hammers and drills. Steel for making pens of the finest quality was a speciality of Jessops and was produced not at their Brightside Works but at the special works in Sheffield, known as the Soho Mills. Their output of steel for pen-making was 1,800 tons per year.

There were two distinct departments at the Brightside Works which were situated on both banks of the River Don and covered forty acres. One dealt with the making of crucible steel, the other with Siemens steel. Crucible steel was produced in melting pots on a comparatively small scale and represented the best quality steel. Siemens steel was produced in large furnaces for castings of up to 50 tons each, for which the finest grades of steel would not be necessary. By the beginning of the twentieth century high quality Jessop steel was produced almost exclusively from iron imported from Sweden, which was of a superior quality to other iron available. They were importing 8,000 tons of it per year.

The crucibles in which crucible steel is made have themselves to be manufactured and part of this process is shown above. Finished crucibles are stacked on shelves awaiting use. In order to make a crucible, different kinds of clay and old crucibles are ground down and mixed together with water in a large trough. It is then kneaded for several hours by men working with their feet. The kneaded clay is cut into lumps of a suitable size, then worked by hand to release any trapped air. After this lump of clay is put into a steel mould or 'flask', a plug is driven down onto it by a hand-worked press. This way the correct thickness and shape of the crucible is achieved. After removal from the mould it is left to dry out and become hard. Once hardened the crucible can withstand the fiercest of fires. A crucible can be used several times over, providing it is never allowed to cool. The fresh crucibles used at Jessops usually lasted for the first three meltings which took place each day. As soon as a crucible cools it cracks and cannot be used again, except for grinding down to mix with the clay to make new crucibles.

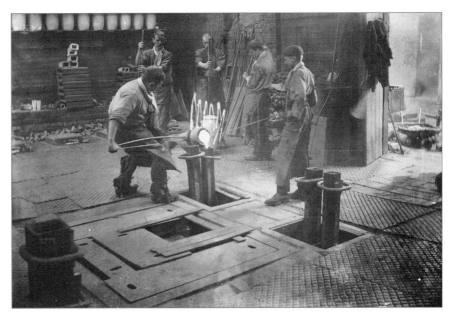

Casting a large crucible steel ingot at William Jessop and Sons Limited.

After treading, the clay is cut into lumps of a suitable size and worked by hand to release any trapped air. This process, known as 'balling' the clay, is shown here at William Jessop and Sons, Brightside Works, *c.* 1904.

A steelworker takes a few moments to slake his thirst at William Jessop and Sons Limited, Brightside Works, during the making of crucible steel, *c.* 1904. Note the protective apron and leggings, in case of hot metal spillage.

Two of Sheffield's great churches. The first photograph shows a view of Ecclesfield, *c.* 1905. Ecclesfield's Parish Church, St Mary's, dominates the centre background. More famously known as 'the Minster of the Moors', St Mary's parish once covered 78 square miles. Although there is evidence of an earlier period of building work in its structure, the church is largely Perpendicular. There is some fine fifteenth and sixteenth century woodwork, including misericord stalls, screens and carved benches, as well as fragments of medieval stained glass. The colours, swords and bugles of the Ecclesfield Volunteers, raised to defend the area from attack by Napoleon, hang on the wall. The church contains a good monument to Sir Richard Scott, who died in 1638. In the churchyard are buried the antiquarian and historian the Revd Joseph Hunter and Alexander John Scott, Chaplain to Lord Nelson at the Battle of Trafalgar, as well as the latter's, his son-in-law, the celebrated Revd Dr Gatty (see page 26).

The medieval church of St Peter, the Parish Church of Sheffield, was rapidly growing short of space by the beginning of the eighteenth century. This prompted the parishioners to organise a public subscription to build a chapel-of-ease nearby. The first stone was laid on 28 May 1720. St Paul's, Pinstone Street, was built to the designs of Ralph Tunnicliffe of Dalton, assisted by John Platt 1 (the elder). It was constructed in the Baroque style of architecture and completed in 1721, although it remained closed for worship for nineteen years, owing to a dispute as to who should appoint the curate. It was one of the finest Georgian buildings in Sheffield. The dome on top of the tower was added in 1769. Sheffield was an archdeaconry within the diocese of York from 1884. After the raising of the parish church to cathedral status in 1914, and owing to the shift of population from the city centre to the suburbs, many city churches became redundant. In 1936 it was decided that some had to be demolished. St Paul's was one of them. The Peace Gardens were created after the Second World War on the site of the church and churchyard, although the removal of human remains did not take place until the new Peace Gardens were laid out in 1998.

A view of LMS Midland Railway station, which opened in 1870, at the turn of the century. As the century closes the facade seen here is still recognisable but the landscape on Park Hill, seen rising behind the station, has altered dramatically. This can be noticed in later views and in particular the last chapter of this book.

Ecclesfield LNER Great Central Railway station, on the Sheffield to Barnsley route, early 1900s. This station also closed in the 1960s as part of the Beeching cuts, as did Ecclesfield Midland Railway station. Now the people of Ecclesfield have to go to neighbouring Chapeltown if they wish to travel by rail into Sheffield.

Wortley Rural District Council's first motor vehicle.

Ecclesfield Handbell Ringers, early 1900s. The landlord of the Greyhound at Ecclesfield, George Hirst, played the concertina and had a keen interest in music generally. After attending a competition in Bradford he came home with a set of handbells. He and a group of friends, which included Tom Kitson and Fred Witham, formed the Ecclesfield Handbell Ringers in 1888. Fred Witham (their leader) is in the centre of the photograph wearing a waistcoat. Ecclesfield Handbell Ringers are still going strong and are a popular attraction wherever they appear.

A group of children pose for the photographer at Crookes, *c.* 1906. Judging by their attire and general demeanour, it must have been a cold day.

The Wicker, looking towards Wicker Arches, *c.* 1907. On the right of the arches is the Great Central Railway's Victoria Station and through the central arch the Midland Railway's goods yard can be seen.

Whenever there was something to celebrate, Sheffield always did it with great style. This photograph shows the first Empire Day celebrations, Bramall Lane, 1906.

Attercliffe Road, *c.* 1905.

Sheffield Wednesday, English Cup winners 1907. Back row (left to right): Messrs. A.G.W. Dronfield, J. Holmes, A.J. Dickinson, J.C. Clegg, H. Nixon, J. Thackray, Ellis, T. Lee, W. Turner, W.F. Wardley. Middle row: Messrs. J. Davis (Assistant Trainer), H. Newbould, H. Davis, Brittleton, Layton, Lyall, Bartlett, Slavin, Burton, Foxall, P. Firth (Trainer). Front row: Messrs. Bradshaw, Chapman, A. Wilson, T. Crawshaw, Stewart, G. Simpson, and Maxwell.

The Church Schools Whitsuntide Parade and gathering, Deepcar, 1907.

A close up view of Ecclesfield's 'the Minster of the Moors', *c.* 1907. Behind the trees on the left can be seen Ecclesfield Vicarage, a large, imposing building, constructed in 1823. The Vicarage was demolished in 1966/7 and replaced by a single storey, flat roofed structure of modern design.

St Mary's Lane, Ecclesfield, *c.* 1908.

The Black Bull, Ecclesfield, *c.* 1908, which was thought to have been built in the sixteenth or seventeenth century. The house on the right was built in 1770. The present public house occupies the entire site.

The following eight postcard views show Ecclesfield Hospital Parade. This was the highlight of the fund-raising year in the village. Before the National Health Service was introduced, hospitals depended heavily on public generosity and the parades were started to collect money for this good cause. The parade took place over the first weekend in July from 1891 to 1936. Horse-drawn carts carried lavishly decorated floats, which were escorted by attendants in fancy dress, carrying collection tins. The floats were made in great secrecy by different communities in the village, hidden from the various competing factions, until the Saturday morning of the parade. These postcard views illustrate just how much effort the people of Ecclesfield put into making each parade a successful and enjoyable event. A group of participants in the 1908 parade pose for the photographer.

The floats usually consisted of a metal or wooden framework, cleverly covered in paper decorations, held together by flour and water paste. After judging, the entire parade toured Sheffield on Saturday afternoon. It went along The Common, up Church Street to Grenoside, down to Wadsley Bridge, past Sheffield Infirmary and across to the bottom of the Moor, up the Moor, along High Street to the Wicker, up to Firth Park, Bellhouse Road, Shiregreen, Hatfield House Lane, down Barnsley Road and back to Stocks Hill. The Mysterious Scareship was one of the floats in the 1909 parade.

The Hospital Sing took place on Sunday afternoon. The parade re-assembled on Monday evening and toured Chapeltown and High Green districts. This float formed part of the 1910 parade.

This entry was in the 1907 parade. The groom is Mr Johnny Parkes. The owner of the cart, Mr Walter Stringer, leans on the cart. His daughter, Bonnie Stringer, and a friend, Miss Salt, are the passengers. Mrs Stringer and her mother-in-law, with Mrs Elliot, the aunt of Mrs Stringer senior, complete the picture.

The Little Mary float from the 1908 parade.

This interesting float appears to be some kind of space ship.

Lady Godiva and Robinson Crusoe's Hut, from the 1910 parade.

This float from the 1912 parade appears to feature a large bird's nest full of little girls.

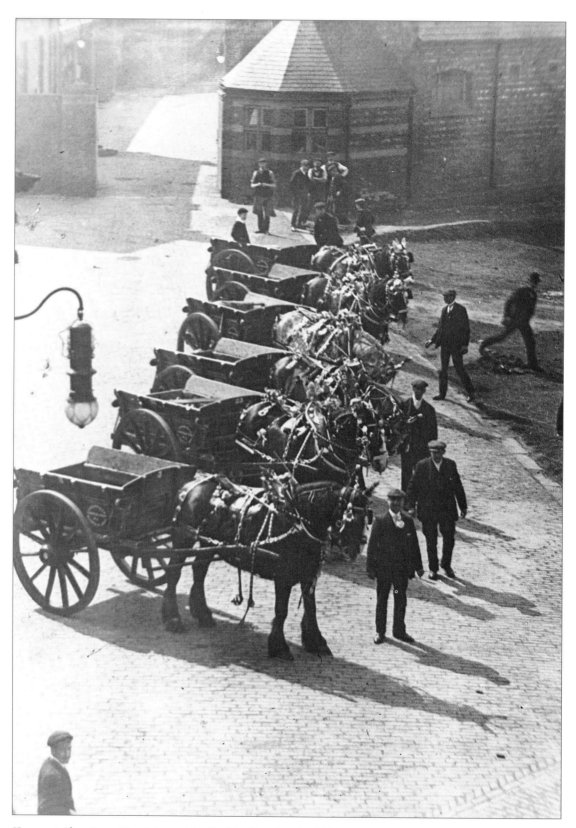

Horses at Olive Grove Depot dressed for the May Day Parade, 1909.

The Civic Service, 14 November 1909, when William Charles de Meuron Wentworth-Fitzwilliam, 7th Earl Fitzwilliam (1872–1943) was Lord Mayor of Sheffield. Lord Fitzwilliam can be seen in his mayoral robes being escorted into Sheffield parish church.

The Grand Hotel, Leopold Street, 1910.

The Wicker, *c.* 1910. A much busier shopping area at the beginning of the century than it is in more recent times.

A 1910 advertisement for Sandfords.

Several views of Hunter's Bar during the Edwardian period.

First World War and the Reign of George V

A postcard showing Ecclesfield Hospital Parade 1911 which depicts a float with a coronation theme. Two kings and queens were used on the different days the parade took place.

A group of Hartley Brook residents outside one of the file cutting shops, *c.* 1911. Among the group are Mr Bill Dawson, Mr Fred Grange and Mrs Spedding.

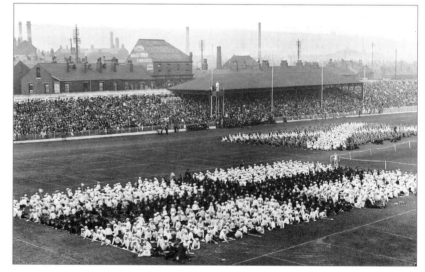

The flags of St George and St Andrew, depicted in the Coronation Pageant, Bramall Lane 1911.

Miners and their wives and children at Candle Main, High Hazels, Darnall (Silkstone Seam), during the coal strike in 1912. This nationwide strike ran from February to April.

The Cinema House, Fargate (later Barker's Pool) opened on 6 May 1913. This advertisement announces the opening. It illustrates the facilities being offered, which would eclipse those of most present-day cinemas.

John Walsh opened his department store in High Street in 1896. This photograph was taken prior to the First World War.

This postcard view of Fargate is stamped 30 January 1914.

The Hospital Sing, Ecclesfield Hospital Parade weekend, 12 July 1914. This postcard view shows the stage erected behind the farm in High Street (now Singletons Transport). Later events were staged behind Bank House (now the Regency Restaurant). Among the artistes are Mrs Clayton, Mrs F. Hallam, Mr H. Gregory, Miss Gregory and Mrs Wright.

Sgt T.A. Bond, No. 6 Platoon, 1st West Riding Divisional Cyclist Company, British Expeditionary Force.

Tinsley Park Colliery FC Sheffield Challenge Cup winners, 1915. Players are, back row: Mr L. Whitney, Mr J. Hartland and Mr J. Wilkinson. Middle row: Mr Stevenson, Mr A. Sheldon and Mr Clarke. Front row: Mr J. Dronfield, Mr A. Denniss, Mr W. Fordie and Mr C. Denton.

War Bonds on sale from a tank parked in Fitzalan Square in 1917.

Peace celebrations in Stocksbridge.

After the Boer War, when the Boers superiority as marksmen was realised, the Government encouraged people to take up shooting and supported the formation of small bore (0.22 inch) rifle clubs. The Ecclesfield Small Bore Rifle and Pistol Club was founded in 1910. Meetings were held in Townend Quarry. The members of the club were known jocularly as the 'Butterfly Shooters', as they rarely hit the target. Back row, left to right: J.H. Butterworth, Moses Yeardley, W. Hinchcliffe, W. Unwin, W.H. Marshall, W. Green, F. Gregory, I. Copley. Front row: J.W. Granger, Mr Kirk, Miss Kirk, F. Robins.

Taken from the junction with Duncan Road, this view shows Crookes in about 1920.

The wedding of Amelia Swift to George Arthur Stables took place on 15 June 1920 at Nether Congregational Church, Norfolk Street. Left to right, standing: Thomas Henry Stables (father of the bridegroom), Reuben Hague (cousin of bride), Thomas William Stables (best man and bridegroom's brother), George Arthur Stables (bridegroom), John Thompson Bellman Swift (bride's father), Mary Alice Dyson (bridegroom's aunt). Seated: Amy Hague (Reuben's daughter), Alice Margery Dyson (bridegroom's cousin), Amelia Swift (bride), Annie Booth Stables (bridegroom's mother), Elsie Fletcher (bride's sister holding baby Winnie).

Samuel Fox & Co., Stocksbridge Works, *c.* 1920.

Cote Lane, Ecclesfield, *c.* 1922. On the right is Ecclesfield Cinema, built in 1920, which seated 685 patrons in stalls and balcony. Built and owned by Michael J. Gleeson, it opened on 1 June 1921 with the film *Broken Blossoms*, starring Lilian Gish. It closed in 1930 for a new sound system to be installed and opened again on 7 March 1932 when *King of Jazz* was screened. The Cinema House was purchased by Essoldo in 1950 and continued to operate until 7 February 1959, when the last film to be shown was *The Young Lions*, starring Marlon Brando.

H.A. Lingard, Ironmongers, Langsett Road, during the 1920s. Among the many goods displayed both in the window and outside the shop is an impressive array of spades, at prices to suit every pocket.

Cole Brothers Ltd was founded in 1847 by three brothers. This photograph shows the famous Sheffield department store in the 1920s. The building was constructed in 1867 and stood at the bottom of Fargate. Cole's Corner was a popular meeting place for a century. These premises were demolished after Cole Brothers moved to new premises in Barker's Pool in 1963.

Whitsuntide Walk, Holy Trinity Church, Darnall, *c.* 1925.

The University of Sheffield's Rag Day, 1926.

Sheffield Wednesday FC League Champions, 1928–29. Back row: Messrs. R. Brown (Secretary), A. Strange, T. Walker, T. Leach, J. Brown, E. Blenkinsop, W. Marsden, F. Craig (Trainer). Front row: Messrs. M. Hooper, J. Seed (Captain), J. Allen, R. Gregg, E. Rimmer.

Sheffield Shelter for Lost and Starving Cats, was founded in 1897 by Miss Jane Barker. It originally operated from Broomspring Lane before moving to Gell Street. The Cats Shelter moved to Travis Place in 1964.

Ecclesfield Whitsuntide Walk, c. 1930, at the corner of High Street and Crow Hill.

This view taken in 1930 shows the City Hall during construction (right foreground), Sheffield Town Hall, the Grand Hotel, Barker's Pool and Surrey Street.

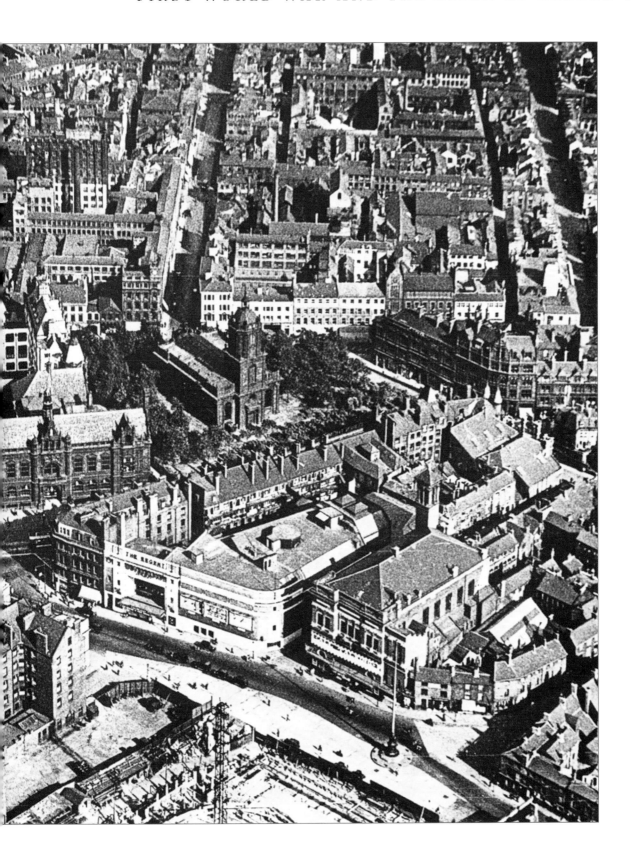

A view taken shortly after the completion of the City Hall. The principal streets shown are Pinstone Street, where the dome and tower of St Paul's Church can be clearly seen, Barker's Pool, Leopold Street and Surrey Street, where work on the Central Library is underway.

The Endcliffe Estate, Fulwood Road, early 1930s.

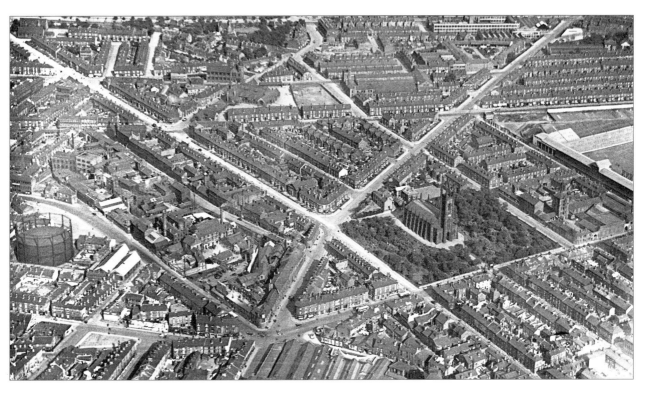

St Mary's Church, Bramall Lane, St Mary's Road and Eyre Street, *c*. 1935.

Abbeydale Road, Abbeydale Cinema, London Road and Chesterfield Road, *c*. 1935.

The Pageant of Sheffield's History, 1931. The Archbishop of York poses with Mary Queen of Scots and other characters from history.

A view of the junction of Barker's Pool and Pinstone Street, *c.* 1935.

A group of Darnall residents relax in Hazel Park, Darnall, after participating in the Whitsuntide parade. A 'stop me and buy one' ice cream cart provides much needed refreshment.

Among the most popular features of the Ecclesfield Hospital Parade were the Plough Bullocks. A plough, supported on a small cart, was pulled through the streets by the willing participants, who were dressed in smocks and driven by a man who smote them at regular intervals with an inflated pig's bladder tied to a cane. A bucket was fastened to the handle of the plough. The ever thirsty Plough Bullocks were refreshed at regular intervals at various public houses on the parade route, when the bucket was filled with ale. In this photograph the Plough Bullocks (pronounced locally Ploo Bullocks) pose for the photographer outside the Ball Inn, Ecclesfield. Mr Alf Ridge (Landlord) of the Ball Inn brings out the much needed refreshment.

Sheffield Wednesday, FA Cup winners 1935. Back row: Tommy Walker, ?, ?, Jack Surtees, Sam Powell (Trainer), Wilf Sharp, Jack Palethorpe, ?, Jackie Robins. Third row: Eric W. Taylor, Ellis Rimmer, Les Fenwick, Jack Brown, Ronnie Starling, Joe Nibloe, Ted Catlin, Walt Millership, George Irwin (Trainer), George Ainsley, Horace Burrows, W.H. Walker (Secretary-manager). Third row: W.F. Warily, E.G. Flint, S.H. Nixon, P. Bowker, W.G. Turner, Sir Charles Clegg, W. Fearnehough, A.J. Blanchard, E. Mills, Dr. Ian Rhind, J. Swallow. Front row: Mark Hooper, ?, Sedley Cooper, Harry Grange, George Drury, Jack Thompson.

The Theatre Royal, Sheffield. This jewel in the crown of Sheffield theatres opened in 1773. It was altered several times and was almost completely rebuilt in 1855. The distinguished and most prolific of theatre architects, Frank Matcham, made alterations to the theatre in 1901. Fire devastated The Theatre Royal during the pantomime season in December 1935. Here firemen try to save the theatre during the disastrous fire which brought about its end. The fire is gradually being brought under control but the stained-glass windows have been blown out, the offices are engulfed in flames and the entire structure of the building has been irretrievably damaged.

Second World War and the Postwar Years

Their Majesties King George VI and Queen Elizabeth visit Sheffield after the December Blitz, January 1941.

The Home Guard being inspected by Lt. General Sir Ronald Adams, in Blonk Street.

Sheffield was blitzed by the Luftwaffe on 12/13 and 15/16 December 1940. This is an aerial view of the city centre following the attacks.

Damage caused to the Empire Theatre and shop property at the junction of Charles Street and Union Street, 12 December 1940. Performances continued at the theatre but the shop premises were never rebuilt. The entire building was demolished in 1959.

A converted Rolls-Royce serves as a WVS mobile canteen, shown here in St Mary's Road, December 1940.

Members of the Central Library staff in the kitchen preparing food for the homeless after the air raids in December 1940. Left to right: Miss J.W. Clare, Miss L. Relph, Miss K.M. Dawes, Miss J.W. Woodward, Miss E.H. Godfrey and a voluntary helper.

Sheffield in flames during the blitz, 15 December 1940.

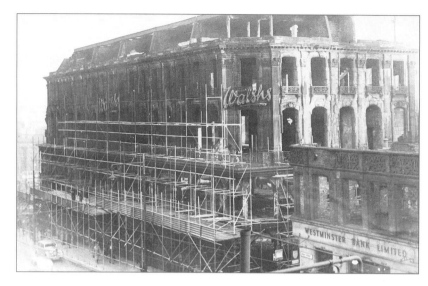

The High Street premises of John Walsh were irreparably damaged during the Sheffield Blitz.

The Prime Minister, Winston S. Churchill, visited Sheffield in November 1941.

A typically Churchillian gesture for the many Sheffield people who came out into the streets to greet the Prime Minister.

Officers of 67th (Sheffield) Battalion West Riding Home Guard.

Attercliffe Road pictured after the end of the Second World War.

The Sheffield Pageant of Production Luncheon, which was held at the Piccadilly Hotel, London, 13 September 1948. Seated at the top table, left to right are: Mr E.W. Senior (Master Cutler), Mr Harold Wilson (President of the Board of Trade), Mr William Yorke (Lord Mayor of Sheffield and Sir Harold West (President of Sheffield Chamber of Commerce).

Sheffield United Cricket Club, 1949. Back row, left to right: Messrs. R. Hall, C. Lee, E. Burgin, J. Ashman, D. Lane, F. Melling and Mr Burgin (Scorer). Front row: Messrs. L. Morgan, C. Turner, K. Lee, R. Douglas and H. Parkin.

Laying the Foundation for Change

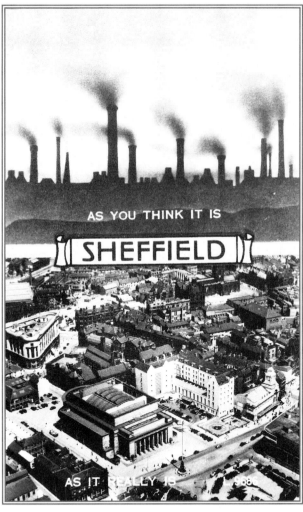

A postcard issued in the 1950s to dispel the myth that Sheffield was a smog-filled city.

Setting circular saws at W. Tyzack & Sons & Turner, April 1950. From front to back: Harry Young, Billy Hance, Bud Wainman, Joe Price, Harry Beaumont (Junior), Leslie Bennett and Alf Linley rolling a saw out.

A view taken of Castle Hill Market and Fitzalan Square in 1950.

Sheaf Market and Sheaf Street, *c.* 1950.

Meadowhead and Abbey Lane junction, 9 February 1952.

The Coronation pageant at Handsworth in 1953, showing the replica crown jewels and regalia.

The Coronation pageant at Handsworth, 1953.

Sheffield city centre in 1954, showing the City Hall, Town Hall with the Peace Gardens to its right, Leopold Street and Surrey Street.

Pond Street, 1956. In the foreground Sheffield College of Technology is under construction. This opened in September 1958. In 1969 the College of Technology merged with the College of Art and one of Britain's first three Polytechnics was created. Following its merger with three teacher colleges in 1976, it was re-named the Sheffield City Polytechnic. In October 1992 Sheffield City Polytechnic was raised to university status and re-named Sheffield Hallam University. Sheffield now has two universities, both with reputations for excellence.

Bill Tomlinson, a long service employee at William Jessop and Sons Limited. The photograph was taken in 1955 on the eve of his 74th birthday. He started work at Jessops at the age of twelve and he said 'I feel I could go on for another 60 years.' His father and grandfather both worked at Jessops. Bill said 'It seemed natural that I should go there too, but my father didn't want that. Anyway, I was determined and as soon as I left Brightside School I presented myself at 7 o'clock one morning at the topside forge. Joe Wade was the manager in those days. He asked me who I was and as soon as he found my father was in his team the job was mine. I had my coat off and was started within 15 minutes.' In addition to his father and grandfather, his brother and two uncles worked there. Two of Bill's cousins Fred and Frank Roper, were also on the payroll. Bill started on 5s. a week (25 pence in today's money), working from 7.00 a.m. to 5.00 p.m. for a five-and-a-half day week.

The newly installed Lord Mayor, Alfred Vernon Wolstenholme JP, visits the famous Sheffield steelworks Firth Brown, 1959.

Swinging '60s and the '70s

Last Tram Week, 2–8 October 1960. Trams ran through the streets of Sheffield and its suburbs from 1873. Sheffield's last tram, Tram No. 510, seen here with its pristine livery, was meant to have been the end of the line for trams in the city. Who could have guessed that they would be introduced to the city streets again within less than forty years?

Tram No. 513 has designs depicting the history of the tram in Sheffield added to its livery, in preparation for last tram week, 1960.

Sheffield's first Christmas illuminations, in Fargate, December 1961.

Cottages in Yew Lane, Ecclesfield, 1964.

Abbeydale Industrial Hamlet, situated between Beauchief and Dore, four miles from the city centre, dates from the eighteenth century and contains workshops, warehouses and cottages. It was once a major agricultural tool-producing concern. Now a museum it has many interesting and important industrial exhibits, such as a crucible furnace, a water-driven tilt forge and grinding wheel and workshops displaying the numerous crafts associated with the hamlet's history.

Walsh's High Street premises, 10 March 1963. This building occupies the site of the original John Walsh department store which was demolished following the Sheffield Blitz. This new store opened in 1953. In the 1970s it became Rackham's and then, in the 1980s, House of Fraser. House of Fraser closed the business in 1998 and an entirely new regime, T.J. Hughes, has been trading from the premises since then.

A view of the junction of Arundel Street and Howard Street, April 1964. The two streets take their names from the Dukes of Norfolk who have been major landowners in Sheffield for centuries.

The Wee Cutlery Shop, Arundel Street, 1965. The shop was established in 1890.

Walsh's department store being altered during the construction of Castle Square (the 'hole in the road'), 30 May 1967.

Sheffield College of Commerce and Technology, Pond Street, December 1964.

Barker's Pool by night. The Gaumont Cinema, which opened in 1927 as the Regent, was re-modelled and re-named in 1969 and can be seen on the right. This attractive cinema was torn down and rebuilt as the multi-screen Odeon in 1987.

The Odeon Cinema, Pond Street, 1968.

A view of the Sunshine Shop, Chapel Walk, by night, 17 October 1969.

Sheffield Polytechnic, Surrey Lane, 1969.

Attercliffe Common at the junction with Steadfast Street, 1970. The car outside the premises formerly occupied by the Blue Heaven Casino, is a Sunbeam Rapier.

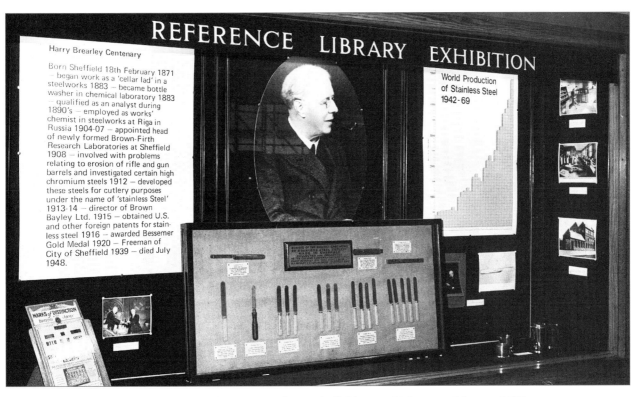

An exhibition celebrating the centenary of Harry Brearley, at Sheffield Central Library in February 1971.

The visit of Her Majesty Queen Elizabeth ll and the Duke of Edinburgh to Sheffield, 29 July 1975. The Lady Mayoress, Mrs Richardson, has her back to the camera.

St Marie's Church, Norfolk Row, before cleaning of the stonework, March 1972. St Marie's was designed by the Sheffield architect M.E. Hadfield and dedicated in 1850. It occupies the site of an eighteenth-century Catholic chapel. St Marie's was upgraded to cathedral status, with Gerald Moverley as its first bishop, when the Roman Catholic Diocese of Hallam was created in 1980.

1980s

The Moor after pedestrianisation, March 1981.

Cole Brothers, Barker's Pool, September 1985. Barker's Pool dates back as far as 1435, when a Mr Barker built a reservoir, which existed until 1793.

Barker's Pool, September 1985. The City Hall can be seen on the right. In the centre background is Sheffield War Memorial.

Mr Mark Briggs of 6 Smelterwood Rise, Sheffield 13, who retired from Allots of Arindel Street on 28 October 1982. This photograph, taken on 28 August 1981, shows Mr Briggs operating the prop hammer.

Midland Railway station, after the façade was cleaned in August 1983. The high rise blocks of Hyde Park dominate the skyline. Compare this view with that on page 38.

The interior of the newly restored Lyceum Theatre in 1990. This beautiful theatre is the only remaining one of the four main theatres in Sheffield, except for the relatively new repertory theatre, the Crucible, built in 1972 and successor to the famous Sheffield Playhouse. Sheffield was on the old No.1 circuit, with no less than three theatres boasting the accolade of being a No.1 theatre, the other circuits being No.2, No.3 and whatever they were, they simply weren't worth mentioning, not least from the artistes' point of view. In the early years of this century, the major venues of over ten theatres were the Alexandra Theatre and Opera House (demolished 1914), the Theatre Royal (Sheffield's magnificent mid-Georgian theatre, destroyed by fire in 1935), Frank Matcham's stupendous Empire Theatre (demolished 1959), Sheffield Hippodrome, built by the celebrated architect Bertie Crewe (opened in 1907 and demolished in 1963) and the Lyceum Theatre. The Lyceum was built on the site of the City Theatre and Circus, which closed after a fire in 1893. This particularly fine replacement was built by W.G.R. Sprague (1865–1933), who was responsible for creating some of the most beautiful theatres in London. Surprisingly, although Sprague has more theatres still standing in London than any other architect, most of which are currently in use, Sheffield's Lyceum is his only work still standing in the provinces. It opened in October 1897, with a performance of *Carmen*, by the Carl Rosa Opera Company, and was a major touring venue for over sixty years. As the popularity of live theatrical performances dwindled in Sheffield, once popular theatres were torn down. By 1966 bingo had replaced live performances at the Lyceum, although the annual pantomime managed to survive until March 1969. Despite mixed fortunes thereafter at the Lyceum, the campaign to save this most deserving theatre succeeded, and one of the most ambitious restoration and regeneration projects ever undertaken on a theatre took place.

A view of the opposite prompt side boxes at the Lyceum Theatre, Sheffield, after restoration in 1990.

Barker's Pool, September 1985. On the right is the Gaumont Cinema, which reopened its doors in 1969, having been re-vamped to replace the Regent, built in 1929. The building was torn down in 1987 and replaced by a multi-screen Odeon complex.

Her Royal Highness Princess Anne on the occasion of her visit to Sheffield on 30 September 1985.

Ponds Forge swimming pool under construction in June 1989. Ponds Forge International Sports Centre is the finest swimming and diving venue in Europe.

The Close of the Twentieth Century

On 3 April 1993, Sheffield's two professional football clubs faced one another in the semi-final of the FA Cup. The match was a great occasion and was held not in Sheffield, but on neutral ground, at the hallowed Wembley Stadium. Wednesday won by two goals to one. Unfortunately, they were beaten in the final by Arsenal.

Among the superb sporting facilities Sheffield built for the World Student Games was the Ponds Forge International Sports Centre in Sheaf Street. Ponds Forge features a super-fast Olympic standard swimming pool and the world's deepest diving pool, as well as the ubiquitous wave machine, lazy river and two 80-metre suspended flumes. There is also a comprehensively equipped sports hall and every conceivable support and relaxation facility for the keen or occasional sporting enthusiast. This view was taken in 1990.

Fitzwilliam Street on 9 December 1991.

The World Student Games were a highly prestigious event and Sheffield took pride in hosting them in 1991. In preparation for this well-attended event, Sheffield upgraded its already excellent sporting facilities, making it a world leader in both the quality and diversity of sporting facilities available within one locality. The scene above is part of the Opening Ceremony at the Don Valley stadium.

The Women's 1500 metres final in the World Student Games at Don Valley Stadium in 1991.

From 1967 until 1994 Sheffield boasted the most extensive network of subterranean tunnels or subways, in any English city. Castle Square, more popularly known as the 'hole in the road', was a particularly fine example of modernist city architecture. From a purely practical point of view the subways enabled shoppers to gain access at basement level to several department stores and shops, and Castle Square in particular, provided a meeting point and a pleasantly appointed place to relax for a few minutes, whilst shopping and to enjoy watching the fish displayed in a large tank. Although Castle Square was a short-lived feature, it is still fondly remembered.

The filling in of Castle Square, Sheffield's fondly remembered 'hole in the road', in preparation for the laying of the tram lines for the Super Tram, in May 1994.

Sheffield Canal Basin in March 1996.

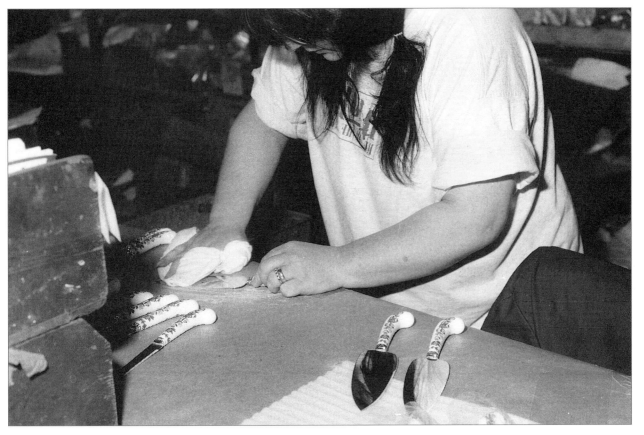

Sheffield still retains its position as a world leader in the production of cutlery. Here the inspection and final polishing of porcelain-handled cake knives is undertaken at Hiram Wild Ltd, in May 1997.

The process, known as 'gigging up', is undertaken at Hiram Wild Ltd, cutlery manufacturers, in May 1997.

Paradise Square, Sheffield. Situated in the heart of the city, this collection of houses are the finest surviving examples of Georgian architecture in Sheffield. Now restored and generally well-maintained, most of these elegant houses are now occupied by solicitors' offices.

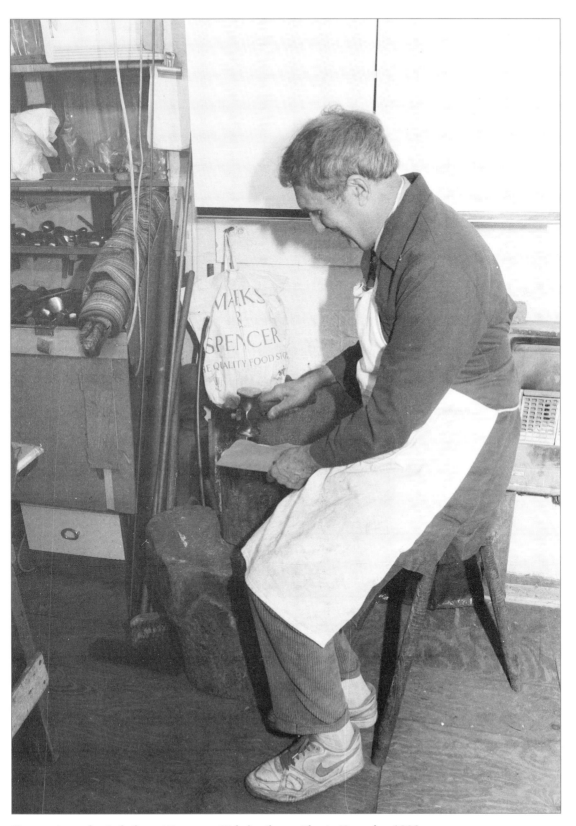

Hammering a sheet of silver at Lawrence Kirby's, silversmiths, in November 1993.

A view of the Lyceum Theatre and the Crucible Theatre in July 1999. The sign of Wards, a famous name in Sheffield's brewing industry since 1890 (although the brewery has older origins under other names), is proudly exhibited in the arched sign to the left of the building. Unfortunately that brewery, together with another famous name in brewing owned by the same conglomerate – that of Vaux of Newcastle-upon-Tyne, was axed when both breweries closed in June 1999. The spire of St Marie's Roman Catholic Cathedral can be seen in the right background.

This view of Arundel Gate in October 1995 shows the fly tower and dressing room block of the Lyceum Theatre on the left, beyond which is the Crucible Theatre. In the distance can be seen the House of Fraser and High Street.

Arundel Gate, October 1995.

A view of Meadowhall which, although by no means the largest, has remained since it opened in September 1990, the most successful shopping complex in Europe. Meadowhall is a large American-style shopping mall, which was built on the site of Hadfield's East Hecla Works. Unlike many such malls, Meadowhall, named after a nearby area, has been tastefully constructed, using high quality materials and incorporating a variety of architectural styles, without adhering to strict principles. The whole effect is extremely pleasing, creating an ambience of quality, without being overwhelming. The result clearly works. Meadowhall exudes quality without intimidating anyone. It caters for a range of shopper from those with just a few pounds to spend to those who have the means to spend the average persons monthly salary on a single purchase.

Meadowhall, July 1999. Meadowhall has over 270 shops and attracts more than 25 million visitors a year. As well as shops, Meadowhall also features an eleven-screen Warner Village cinema complex.

Barker's Pool in July 1999. Sheffield's distinctive war memorial, with its tall flagpole, is in the foreground. The hi-tech shops to the right of Cole Brothers have recently been built on the site of the Odeon Complex, which opened in 1987, replacing the Gaumont Cinema which opened in 1969 on the site of the 1927 Regent Cinema.

A view of Park Hill flats from Arundel Gate, taken in July 1999. Hyde Park flats can be seen looming above Sheffield Midland railway station, the façade of which has remained largely unchanged since the station opened in 1870.

113

Park Hill flats and Hyde Park flats from Arundel Gate, July 1999. Park Hill flats were designed in the late 1950s and first occupied in 1961. The innovative design of this 'village in the sky', inspired by Le Corbusier, encouraged the construction of similar, although largely less successful, complexes throughout the United Kingdom. The flats were accessible by lifts and attractive, unusually wide, pedestrian walkways. Household refuse was put to good use by being burned in a central incinerator to provide central heating. Shops, a laundrette and almost everything one would expect to find in a village community were included in the complex. Unfortunately, the Hyde Park estate, located on an adjacent site, did not reach the same degree of success with its high rise blocks.

The curious eggbox-like extension to Sheffield Town Hall built between 1973 and 1977, photographed from the Peace Gardens, July 1999.

The Crucible Theatre, July 1999. One of England's finest repertory theatres, it is known to a wider audience via television as the venue for the World Snooker Championships.

The Peace Gardens July 1999. A plaque proclaims that the cascades are dedicated to the memory of the Sheffield Chartist Leader, Samuel Holberry (1814–1842).

An interesting view of the fountains and cascades in the Peace Gardens, July 1999.

The Super Tram passes the Cathedral Church of St Peter and St Paul. The 1960s extension to the cathedral can be seen on the left.

Looking down the Moor from Pinstone Street, July 1999.

Park Square viewed from Sheaf Market, July 1999.

A 1999 view of the beautifully restored Sheffield Canal Basin, which was re-named Victoria Quays.

Sheffield City Council invested £10 million in restoring Victoria Quays. What for many years was a dilapidated complex of waterside buildings has become one of the most attractive features in the city.

Victoria Quays in July 1999, looking towards the city centre.

Acknowledgements and Picture Credits

Thanks are due to the following individuals and companies for their assistance during the production of this book.

My personal assistant Mr John D. Murray, Mr Paul T. Langley Welch, for his contribution in bringing the photographic history of Sheffield right up to date. Mr Cyril Slinn for use of part of his photographic archive and his own personal photographs, as well as his assistance in providing factual information concerning various subjects. Mr Herbert and Mrs Doreen Howse, Mr Clifford and Mrs Margaret Willoughby, Mr David and Mrs Christine Walker of Walkers Newsagents, Hoyland, Mr Doug Hindmarch, Senior Local Studies Librarian at Sheffield Central Library and the staff of Sheffield central Library Local Studies Department, Mr Stables, Miss Tracy P. Deller, Mrs Sylvia Steel, Miss Joanna C. Murray Deller, Ricki S. Deller, J.A. Walker, Mr Simon Fletcher, Annabel Fearnley, Fiona Eadie and Olwen Greany.

All photographs are from the Sheffield City Library collection with the exception of the following (all numbers given are page numbers): Cyril Slinn collection: frontispiece, half-title page, 8, 24, 25 bottom, 32, 33 both, 34, 36, 39 both, 43 both, 44 both, 45 both, 46 all, 47 both, 51, 52 top, 54 bottom, 55 top, 57 bottom, 59 bottom, 63 bottom, 69 bottom, 87 top; Paul T. Langley Welsh: 6, 11; Doreen Howse collection: 20 middle, 21 bottom, 22 top, 40 both, 52 bottom, 58 top, 63 top; Author's collection: 31; by Paul T. Langley Welch 18, 110 top, 111 bottom, 112, 113 both, 114 both, 115 both, 116 both, 117 both, 118–19, 120 both.